Mickey Mantle

Howard Weinstein

the rosen publishing group's
rosen
central

Thanks to my older brother Marc, who introduced me to baseball (even if he was a Dodgers fan!)

Published in 2004 by The Rosen Publishing Group, Inc.
29 East 21st Street, New York, NY 10010

First Edition

Library of Congress Cataloging-in-Publication Data

Weinstein, Howard.
Mickey Mantle / Howard Weinstein.— 1st ed.
    p. cm. — (Baseball Hall of Famers)
Summary: Describes the life and career of the New York Yankees star famed for his legendary hitting ability.
Includes bibliographical references and index.
ISBN 0-8239-3782-8 (lib. bdg.)
1.   Mantle, Mickey, 1931–1995—Juvenile literature. 2. Baseball players—United States—Biography—Juvenile literature. 3. New York Yankees (Baseball team)—Juvenile literature. [1. Mantle, Mickey, 1931–1995. 2. Baseball players.] I. Title. II. Series.
GV865.M33 W45 2003
796.357'092—dc21

                                                      2002010755

Manufactured in the United States of America

Contents

Mickey Mantle poses during spring training in 1951 at the age of nineteen. The patch on the left shoulder of his uniform marks the American League's 50th anniversary.

Introduction

Although many great athletes are described as "born to play" their chosen sport, often the description is an exaggeration. In Mickey Mantle's case, it's close to the truth. His father named him after Mickey Cochrane, a hard-hitting catcher for the Philadelphia Athletics. Mantle's mother remembered her husband's disappointment when his day-old son preferred a warm bottle to a baseball.

By day, Mantle's father worked in the Oklahoma mines, but his nights were spent dreaming of a better life for his son—as a major league ballplayer. As soon as Mickey was old enough to swing a bat, his father began pitching baseballs to him. Eventually, Mickey more than fulfilled his father's hopes, becoming

Mickey Mantle

This is the first Mickey Mantle baseball card, issued in 1952 while he was a rookie. This card has sold to collectors at prices as high as $50,000. One of the most prized cards a collector can own, it features original artwork and a facsimile of Mickey's signature.

the star center fielder of the legendary New York Yankees. During Mantle's first fourteen seasons with the team, the Yankees won twelve pennants and seven championships. He hit more home runs than any switch-hitter in history, and set World Series records that may stand forever.

To many, Mantle's life seems like the American dream come true—from miner's son to Baseball Hall of Fame legend. But serious leg injuries nearly ended his career before it began, and he never played without pain. A family history of cancer and a fear of dying young pushed him to live with a reckless intensity that hurt both his career and his health. If he'd known that he was going to live that long, Mantle joked on his fiftieth birthday, he'd have taken better care of himself.

Few athletes have been more admired for their on-field courage. Few players tried harder to help their teams win. For these reasons, millions of fans consider Mantle a hero for his athletic accomplishments. Yet Mantle thought himself a failure for his personal flaws.

In the end, he showed a different and more important kind of courage—making amends for his mistakes, facing death with honesty and dignity, and becoming a true hero.

The Mick flashes a grin in this photo from 1966.

Baseball in His Blood

Mickey Charles Mantle was born on October 20, 1931, in a two-room house on a dirt road in Spavinaw, Oklahoma. His father, Elvin, had been nicknamed "Mutt" as a baby, and that's what everyone called him. His mother, Lovell, was several years older than her husband, and she had been previously married and divorced.

Mickey was their first child together, born just after the Great Depression began. Money was hard to come by in those days, and unemployment was rampant. In the dust bowl of the Great Plains, years of drought and poor soil conservation led to huge dust storms, forcing many farmers to leave town and head west in search of jobs to support their families.

Spavinaw was a small town in northeastern Oklahoma, near the Kansas and Missouri borders. Thanks to rich lead and zinc deposits deep underground, the mining industry provided steady, but hazardous, employment. After Mickey's birth, his family moved to the nearby town of Commerce, and Mutt started working at the Eagle-Picher mines.

If mining was Mutt's livelihood, baseball was his life. Most of the mines had semi-professional teams, and Mutt played games every weekend. In the evenings he'd bring home broken bats and cut them down to a child's size. His work was exhausting, but he still practiced baseball with Mickey every day. Mickey's grandfather Charlie also joined in, taking turns pitching. By the time Mickey was four years old, he was learning to switch-hit—to bat from either side of the plate—a skill that gives hitters an advantage over other players who hit only from the left or the right.

Lovell shared her husband's love of baseball, and both rooted for the nearest big-league team, the St. Louis Cardinals. She'd listen

Mantle *(right)* chats with his father, Elvin *(left)*, and former Yankee Cliff Mapes *(center)* at one of the Commerce, Oklahoma, lead and zinc mines.

to Cardinals games on the radio while doing housework and made Mickey's toddler clothing from Mutt's old baseball uniforms. Although there was little money to spare, each Christmas marked a moment when Mickey received a new baseball glove.

For Mickey, there was no such thing as too much baseball. When he wasn't practicing with his father and grandfather, he'd play with friends on dusty fields near abandoned mineshafts. By

The Mantle family enjoys a card game at home in Commerce in 1951. Pictured from left to right are his brother Roy, Mickey, his mother, his brother "Butch" (Larry), his father, and his brother Ray.

their early teens, he and his friends played on a local sandlot team against teenagers from other mining towns.

In 1944, when Mickey was thirteen years old, Grandpa Charlie became sick, the first Mantle to develop a cancer called Hodgkin's disease. Mutt moved the family to a farm outside of Commerce, hoping that fresh air would improve his father's health, but Charlie soon died.

Afterward, the Mantle family stayed on the farm for a while. Mickey and his younger twin brothers Ray and Roy, his sister Barbara, and his youngest brother Butch helped with chores. On the farm there was plenty of room for family games of baseball and football. Sometimes, Mickey even rode a horse to school. And though money remained scarce, Mutt seemed happier working outdoors on the farm than he had been down in the mine shafts.

But just before harvest season, heavy rains wiped out the year's crops. Without much money, the Mantles packed their belongings and moved again—this time to the tiny town of Whitebird, just outside Commerce. Their house was little more than a shack, without indoor plumbing. Mutt reluctantly returned to work in the mines.

A Nightmare Injury

Though not a great student, Mickey passed all his classes. He even became sports editor of the Commerce High newspaper. But he was more interested in playing sports than writing about them. In tenth grade, he joined the football team. Mutt's worst fears about injuries came true when Mickey got kicked in the left shin during football practice. By the next morning, he had a high fever and his ankle was badly swollen. He was diagnosed with osteomyelitis, a serious infection of the bone marrow.

After two weeks without improvement, Mantle's parents drove him 175 miles (282 kilometers) to a larger hospital in Oklahoma City, where doctors wanted to amputate his leg. Lovell refused to allow it. Instead, doctors tried penicillin, a new antibiotic at the time. For days, he was given injections every three hours. The penicillin worked, the infection improved, and Mickey finally went home.

After months spent recovering the weight and strength lost during his ordeal, Mickey joined the Commerce High basketball team. The following summer, Mantle again played baseball for a local sandlot team. This time, he played second base. One day, Mickey's team played the highest-ranked team in the region— the Whiz Kids from Baxter Springs, Kansas.

Mantle's hitting skills and speed impressed the Baxter Springs manager, Barney Barnett.

Like Mutt, Barnett worked at the mines and loved baseball. He had helped organize the Ban Johnson League, which was a step up from sandlot ball. Ban Johnson players were the area's best athletes and big-league scouts searching for promising youngsters often came to Baxter Springs games. Though he'd be one of the youngest players in the league, Mantle was thrilled when Barnett invited him to join his team.

Getting Noticed

The following summer, sixteen-year-old Mickey played shortstop for the Whiz Kids and strengthened his muscles working as a cemetery gravedigger. The Ban Johnson team regularly drew a few hundred spectators, sometimes during the night with the ballpark lit brightly for games, unusual for a small-town team. The local paper, *The Joplin Globe*, often covered the game. The Spring River flowed past the outfield, 400 feet (122 meters) away in center—roughly the distance to the center-field fence in major league ballparks.

Mantle chats with Yankee scout Tom Greenwade in this photo from April 1951.

One day, when New York Yankee scout Tom Greenwade came to watch another Whiz Kids player, Mantle slugged two home runs out to the river. Later that day, when a rainstorm drenched the ballpark, Mutt brought Mickey to the family car—where Greenwade waited inside. Much to Mickey's astonishment, Greenwade asked him if he'd like to play for the Yankees. Since Mantle wasn't yet seventeen years of age, Greenwade couldn't sign him until he graduated high school the following spring. As Mantle recalled, Greenwade promised he'd return on Mickey's graduation day.

Other recollections of the meeting differ from Mantle's, but all end the same way. The night of Mickey's graduation in May 1949, the Whiz Kids had a game in Coffeyville, Kansas. Since Mickey already had his diploma, he skipped the graduation ceremony to play baseball instead—with Greenwade watching. By the end of that weekend, Mickey had signed with the Yankees for $1,500 in salary and bonus—not much by today's standards, but Mantle was on his way to realizing his dream.

2 Minors to Majors

Fresh from his high school graduation, Mickey, not yet an adult, was about to play professional baseball. He reported to manager Harry Craft at New York's Independence, Kansas, Class D farm team in the Kansas-Oklahoma-Missouri League, marking the bottom of the professional baseball ladder. If young players advance at all, most of them climb one difficult step at a time, facing the toughest competition of their lives. Every game, pitch, and at-bat carries more importance than ever before. How well they play—and learn—will determine how far they will rise in their athletic careers. Few players make the big leagues. It is unlikely that anyone could have predicted just how quickly Mickey would reach Yankee Stadium.

At first, Mantle was so homesick he considered returning to the Commerce sandlots and a job in the Oklahoma mines. Since most of his peers were also young, Mickey soon formed friendships, rooming with teammates in a house owned by an elderly couple. When they weren't playing or practicing ball, they'd be snacking and girl-watching at a local hangout.

Back at the ballpark, Mantle had to learn a tough lesson—that even a .300 batter fails to hit seven out of every ten tries. "Sometimes, after a strikeout, feeling . . . mad at myself," he wrote in his autobiography, *The Mick*, "I'd trot off the field and let loose a vicious kick at the dugout water cooler." Once, he kicked it so hard that it sprung a leak, with water gushing 5 feet (1.52 meters) in the air. Afterwards, his teammates nicknamed him "King of the Broken Water Coolers."

Meanwhile, at shortstop, Mantle made 47 errors in 89 games. He had trouble catching high pop-ups, and his wild throws to first base often sailed into the stands. But he batted .313, with 63 runs batted and 54 runs scored. The Independence Yankees won their league championship.

Meeting Merlyn

After the season, Mantle worked at the mines as an electrician's helper, and relaxed with his old friends. One Friday night, at the big high school football game between Commerce and Picher, they noticed a pair of Picher majorettes. Always a shy youth, Mickey relied upon his friends to arrange a triple date. When Mickey finally asked his date to go out again, she was busy. Finally, he mustered his courage and called one of the other girls instead—Merlyn Johnson. She said yes, even though she already had a boyfriend. At first, she dated both boys, but soon chose Mickey. "He was just as shy as I was, maybe more, and I liked that about him," Merlyn wrote in the Mantle family memoir, *A Hero All His Life*. "He always smelled good, and he had a fresh and outdoorsy look . . . We never touched a drop of alcohol on our dates." Before long, they were going steady.

Mantle poses with his girlfriend, Merlyn Johnson, during a game in 1951.

In November 1949, the local military draft board called Mantle for a mandatory physical. Because of the chronic bone infection in his left leg, he was classified 4-F, or ineligible for military service.

In 1950, Mantle and many of his teammates from Independence played for the Joplin Miners, the Yankees' Class C team in the Western Association. Once again, the team was managed by Harry Craft. All the Yankee farm teams first gathered at a preseason training camp in the Ozark Mountains near Branson, Missouri—and the Miners beat them all, even the top Triple A teams.

When the regular season began, the Miners tore through the Western Association, and Mantle soon became known as one of their star players. Though still baby-faced, his shoulders and back were muscular and he hit with astounding power.

The "Commerce Comet"

After one of Mantle's home-run balls flew over the center-field fence, Joplin's equipment manager called it the longest drive he'd seen since Babe Ruth cleared the roof at Sportsman's Park in St. Louis during the 1928 World Series. And though that may have been the first time anyone had measured Mantle against the Babe, it wouldn't be the last.

Local restaurants sponsored the team's radio broadcasts and awarded free steak dinners for two to any Joplin player hitting a home run. Mantle ate plenty of steak that season. Noting his power, speed, and batting average close to .400, the local papers called him "the Commerce Comet." Craft's reports to Yankee executives gave Mantle top ratings for hitting and running—and suggested switching him from shortstop to a position in the outfield.

At the league's All-Star game, however, Mantle made four errors. Then, late in the game, when the infielders whipped the ball "around the horn" from one to the other before tossing it back to the pitcher, the third baseman's throw to shortstop Mantle hit him right in the face. As Mantle said later, his timing hadn't quite caught up with his strength.

Though Joplin lost in the playoffs, Mantle had a great year, leading the league with a .383 average, 199 hits, and 141 runs scored. He pounded 26 home runs and drove in 136 runs. Though he also made 55 errors, he was rewarded with a surprise call-up from the Yankees.

New York's regular season was nearly finished. It was unlikely that Mantle would even play, so he expected to spend another year in the minors. But for two weeks, he'd be wearing Yankee pinstripes and living his dream.

Once Mantle met the team in St. Louis, he dressed in the same locker room as Yankee All-Stars and veterans. He watched young players already making their mark, including Yogi Berra and Whitey Ford. And he was in awe of the biggest star of all, Joe DiMaggio.

DiMaggio was considered baseball royalty, a man who had played center field for the Yankees with unsurpassed skill and grace since 1936. Off the field, he was reserved and aloof, even with long-time teammates. The shy kid from Oklahoma was too terrified to even say hello to the "Yankee Clipper."

The New York Yankees' legendary outfielder Joe DiMaggio, one of the greatest baseball players of all time, prepares to smack the ball in this photo from 1945.

Even as Mantle observed the finer points of the game, he doubted he'd ever be good enough to make the majors. "I knew manager Casey Stengel had released a statement saying I was the Yankees' number one prize," Mantle wrote in *The Mick*. "Just then I felt like their booby prize."

For the season's final weeks, Mantle roomed with another rookie, Bill "Moose" Skowron. They practiced together, watched

In this photo from 1955, Yankee players Mickey Mantle, Bill Skowron, and Phil Rizzuto examine Rizzuto's cracked plastic helmet, which saved him from injury when he was beaned.

games together, and quickly became friends. When the season ended, they each returned home. The Yankees went on to sweep the World Series from the Philadelphia Phillies, winning their second consecutive world championship.

Once back in Oklahoma, Mickey took a full-time job at the mines, and he and Merlyn continued dating. Mutt hoped they would soon get married. Proud of his son's progress, he worried about big-city temptations that might distract Mickey from baseball if he remained single. A wife and a family might help his son mature a bit faster, his father reasoned. And Mutt couldn't wait to have a grandson.

Over that winter, Mutt seemed very tired. Still, with his father insisting he was fine, Mickey went off to Yankee training camp. Boarding a train for Arizona in 1951, he said good-bye to his parents at the station.

Countless boys have started out as Mantle had, hitting tennis balls and dreaming of becoming ballplayers. Unlike most boys, though, Mantle had both talent and determination. As the train rolled west through Oklahoma, New Mexico, and Arizona, Mantle was heading for an uncertain destiny.

Next Stop . . . New York?

As training camp got underway, Mantle soon stunned manager Casey Stengel with his speed. Whenever ballplayers ran 50-yard (46-meter) races, Mantle always won. When Stengel clocked Mantle around the bases, he'd never seen anyone run faster.

Taking Craft's advice, the Yankees moved Mantle from his position as shortstop to one in the outfield. In his first game there, he tried to catch a line-drive hit headed directly at him. An instant after he flipped his sunglasses down, the ball hit him on the forehead. He wasn't badly hurt, but his teammates couldn't help laughing.

At bat, he slugged long home runs, and his outfield play improved. He was fast enough to catch balls other outfielders couldn't reach. And he learned to make bullet throws, gunning out surprised base runners who didn't know what to expect from the unknown rookie. The news of Mantle's talents spread like wildfire.

Brooklyn Dodgers president Branch Rickey thought that Mantle was the best prospect he'd ever seen. Casey Stengel said, with only slight exaggeration, that Mantle could hit balls over buildings. When training camp ended, Mantle stayed with the major league club, though he modestly expected to be assigned to a farm team for the 1951 season.

During an exhibition game at the University of Southern California's Bovard Field, Mantle

Dodgers president Branch Rickey goes to the locker room to congratulate his team for beating the Yankees 1–0 in Game 2 of the World Series on October 6, 1949.

thrilled the crowd with a single, a triple, and two homers. The first home run hit the roof of a house 600 feet (183 meters) away. The second went even farther, rocketing over the fence, crossing a football field, and landing an astounding 656 feet (200 meters) from home plate, quite possibly the longest home run ever hit. After the game, screaming fans mobbed Mantle. They gathered around the rookie player, clamoring for autographs. At the age of nineteen, Mantle got a taste of the scarier side of athletic stardom.

Then, much to his surprise, a new letter came from the Oklahoma draft board. Since his original medical deferment, the Korean War had begun. Halfway around the world, allied troops were engaged in combat against Chinese and North Korean armies trying to conquer South Korea. Many Americans were drafted, and Mantle certainly seemed as healthy as any one of them. His 4-F status drew complaints from draft officials. Mantle even started getting mail calling him a coward. The Yankees hoped another medical exam would end the controversy. If his status changed, Mantle would have been proud to serve. But the medical judgment remained the same. Osteomyelitis again disqualified Mantle from military service.

On that trip home, Mantle saw that his father looked worse than he had just two months before. Mickey felt certain there was something seriously wrong, but Mutt dismissed his concerns and sent him back to the Yankees in time for a preseason game against the Dodgers in Brooklyn.

With three major league teams—the Yankees, Dodgers, and Giants—New York was a baseball lover's paradise in those days. Loyalties divided neighborhoods—and even families—all over the city, as fans debated whose favorite team was the best.

But there was a special rivalry between the Dodgers and Yankees, a team that had dominated baseball since the 1920s. The Dodgers had often played well, only to end up as heartbreaking losers. Brooklyn fans kept the faith by bravely declaring "Wait 'til next year!" at the end of each disappointing season.

Mantle, already baseball's most talked-about rookie, played like a superstar at Ebbets Field, with a home run among his four hits. He finished spring training batting .402. Stengel knew he wanted Mantle playing for the Yankees, not in the minors. Team president George Weiss resisted, but Stengel prevailed. On the team train to Washington, D.C., for opening day against the Senators, Stengel first told Mantle he'd be starting the year with the defending world champions.

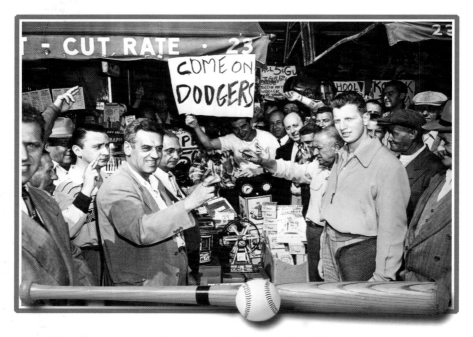

New Yorkers crowd the streets on September 26, 1951, as the Brooklyn Dodgers defend their championship in Boston. The Dodgers beat the Boston Braves 15–5 that day. The Yankees and Dodgers were longtime rivals.

Stengel, a shrewd forty-year veteran of the game—both as player and manager—thought it would be less intimidating for Mantle to make his debut on the road rather than at Yankee Stadium. Unfortunately, the games were rained out and the Yankees returned to New York. Mantle's first game would be before a demanding home crowd in the nation's most famous stadium.

Ghosts on the Field

Mantle was a teenage slugger with blazing speed, joining a team with a history unmatched in American sports. The city's newspapers even hailed him as the next in a line of Yankee superstars dating from at least thirty years before. Mantle faced unbearable pressure to succeed.

Home-run king Babe Ruth led the Yankees to their first championship in 1923. The team then became known as the "Bronx Bombers," and Yankee Stadium was called the "House that Ruth Built." In 1925, first baseman Lou Gehrig joined Ruth. From 1926 to 1934, they led the Yanks to four American League pennants and three World Series victories. By 1935, Ruth was gone. Young Joe DiMaggio joined the team in 1936, and he and Gehrig led the Yankees to three straight championships. Even after a fatal illness struck

Gehrig, DiMaggio's Yankees won seven more pennants and six World Series.

Now, Mantle's first season would be DiMaggio's last. Ready or not, Mantle had been anointed as the next Yankee superstar. As if to emphasize that point, he wore uniform number six, next in line after Ruth's three, Gehrig's four, and DiMaggio's five.

Taking to the diamond on opening day, Mantle heard the roar of 50,000 fans. He felt the ghosts of Ruth and Gehrig with him on that hallowed field of dreams. In the sixth inning, Mantle got his first major league hit, driving in a run with a solid single.

Up and Down . . . and Up

But Mantle wasn't Ruth, Gehrig, or DiMaggio. He was a rookie, and opposing pitchers quickly discovered that he couldn't hit high-inside fastballs when batting lefty. To stop the talented ballplayer, they threw those fastballs again and again. Mantle soon learned how loyal fans could become nasty. They booed when he struck out, and called him a bum when he returned to right field. Sportswriters turned from sugary praise to bitter criticism. By the end of April, Mantle had no home runs and wondered if he'd ever hit one again.

He finally did, on May 1—a 450-foot drive in Chicago. But his slump continued. Mantle's increasing anxiety worsened his ability to play ball. As his frustration boiled over, Mantle started smashing bats, kicking chairs, and even pounding his fists on the dugout roof. And nothing had prepared him for the daily post-game ordeal of dealing with the press. Reporters surrounded him at his locker and fired questions at him about every strikeout.

Despite Stengel's encouragement, Mantle repeatedly made the same mistakes. When Stengel's patience diminished, he began benching his rookie. Finally, by mid-July, he tearfully told Mantle he was being sent to the minors to regain his confidence. Mantle felt crushed. He'd come so far, only to fail during his first season.

He joined the Triple-A Kansas City Blues, but his slump worsened. After twenty-one consecutive hitless at-bats, he called his father. Mantle was ready to give up. At this, Mutt and Merlyn made the tiring five-hour drive from Commerce to Mickey's Kansas City hotel room.

Instead of sympathy, Mantle wrote in *The Mick*, he saw anger and disappointment in his father's eyes. Mickey told his father that it was no use; he just couldn't hit any more. "Shut up!" Mutt snapped. "I don't want to hear that whining. I thought I raised a man, not a coward!"

Mutt started packing his son's suitcase. If Mickey couldn't play ball, he'd come back to the Oklahoma mines. Mickey pleaded for another chance.

His hitting quickly improved. In 40 games with Kansas City, he hit 11 home runs, drove in 50 runs, and batted .361. The Yankees recalled him in August. And he was given a new number, with which he would be forever identified—seven.

Sharing a Manhattan apartment over the famous Stage Deli with teammates Johnny Hopp and Hank Bauer, the country kid discovered New York City. The longer he lived there, the more he liked the excitement it offered.

Mantle strikes a defensive pose at spring training during his rookie year. Though he would fold under pressure and be sent back to the minors, it was a crucial learning experience for the talented, but then unproven, young player.

The Yankees clinched the 1951 pennant. In two-thirds of a season, Mantle batted .267, hit 13 home runs, and drove in 65 runs—just a taste of the talents he had in store.

Triumph . . . and Tragedy

Anxious to see Mickey play in the World Series, Mutt drove to New York with two friends. Mantle was shocked to see that his father had lost 30 pounds (14 kg) since midsummer. Mutt looked sick, but he wanted to enjoy his first trip to New York. He and his pals saw one of the most exciting games in baseball history. The Dodgers and Giants had tied for first place, and in the last of a special three-game playoff, Giants third baseman Bobby Thomson dashed the Dodgers' hopes with a bottom-of-the-ninth home run to win the pennant. The Dodgers were now destined to go on to the World Series against the Yankees.

In the first two games at Yankee Stadium, Mantle batted leadoff and played right field. DiMaggio, playing with a heel injury, could no longer cover center-field, so Stengel told Mantle to cover the right center-field gap.

After the Giants won the first game, the Yanks led 2–0 in Game 2. In the sixth inning, the Giants' rookie center fielder, Willie Mays, flared a fly ball to short right-center. Mantle ran over to cover for DiMaggio. At the last instant, DiMaggio called Mantle off and prepared to make the catch himself. As Mantle swerved to avoid colliding with DiMaggio, his spikes caught on a sprinkler-drain cap embedded in the grass. Mantle's right knee twisted horribly and he collapsed. He was carried off on a stretcher, his season now over.

The next morning, he and his father took a cab to Lenox Hill Hospital. But as Mickey leaned on his father for support, Mutt collapsed. Father and son shared a hospital room and watched the World Series together on television. Shortly after Mickey's operation to repair torn knee ligaments, he was told that his father had Hodgkin's disease. Mutt was dying.

After the Yankees beat the Giants without him, Mickey bought his family a comfortable house in Commerce, Oklahoma. And he and Merlyn got married on December 23, 1951—the best Christmas present he could give his father.

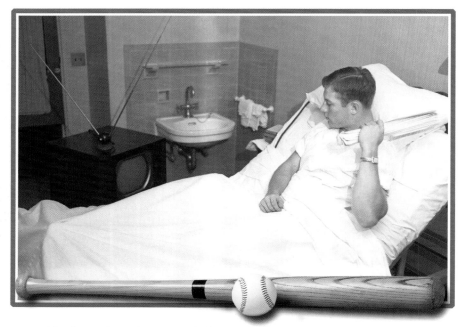

Mantle watches television in the hospital room he shared with his father when both were laid up during the 1951 World Series.

Yet, even as he faced some adult responsibilities, he ignored others—including the doctor's prescribed exercises to strengthen his right knee. "I thought the muscles would automatically come back, [as] good as ever," he wrote in *The Mick*. "I was twenty [years old] . . . and I thought I was a superman."

That winter, Mickey and Merlyn drove Mutt to the Mayo Clinic in Minnesota, where doctors confirmed that his cancer was terminal.

Mickey tried to cope with his sorrow. For the first time, he sought escape by drinking alcohol. But nothing could make his father well. In 1952, when Mantle reported to spring training in Florida, he was still recovering from knee surgery. Stengel started him in right field.

Shadowed by Death

Mutt died on May 6, 1952. Although he'd lived long enough to see his son play ball for the world champion Yankees, he was only thirty-nine years old, his life shortened by ravenous illness. Mickey felt bitterly angry at God. He played in the Yankees game the day his father died, believing that's what Mutt would have wanted.

Mantle returned to Oklahoma for his father's funeral. At the graveside, he thought of all the chances he'd had to tell his father how much he loved him, but never did. And now his father's firm guiding hand was gone forever.

That same year, Mutt's youngest brother Emmett died at thirty-two, also of Hodgkin's disease. Mutt's middle brother, Tunney, had died several years before, at thirty-four. Because his grandfather, father, and two uncles had all died of cancer, Mantle began to believe that he, too, would also die young.

Late that May, Mantle finally took DiMaggio's place in center-field and started hitting with authority. He also became "road roommates" (during away games) with a hot-tempered rookie second baseman named Billy Martin. They and their wives also shared a New York apartment. Martin had grown up as a city kid in Oakland, California—quite unlike Mantle, a country boy from Oklahoma. Despite their differences, Mantle and Martin became friends. They also became drinking buddies, often staying out late at bars, then sneaking back to their hotel room to avoid Stengel's wrath.

The Yankees won the 1952 pennant. Mantle batted .311, with 37 doubles, 23 homers, and 87 runs batted in. The Yanks played another "Subway Series," this time against the Dodgers. After five games, the Dodgers led the series 3-2. Dodger fans could taste victory, but Mantle hit home runs to help

The Mantles and Martins pose with Yankee Yogi Berra *(center)* during a theater event in June 1956.

the Yankees win both games—and their fourth straight championship.

Back in Commerce, Mantle was honored with a parade and a banquet. His only regret was that his father couldn't be there. "No thrill ever seemed bigger or more rewarding," he wrote in *The Mick.* "Somehow the wins seemed to get less and less exciting as the years went by. This was special . . . How many times can you feel the same intensity as the first time?"

4 Achieving Greatness

Mantle was an important part of a team trying to win five consecutive World Series—something no team had ever done before. Although he showed flashes of greatness, it wasn't enough for some fans and sportswriters who continued to make unfair comparisons between Mantle and DiMaggio, Ruth, and Gehrig. When Mantle hit long home runs, they complained that he didn't hit enough of them. With all his natural ability, it was easy to forget he was only twenty-one years old, certainly still developing his skills as a ballplayer. He and Martin often behaved like teenagers, pulling clubhouse pranks and chasing each other with water pistols.

Mantle had a complex relationship with Casey Stengel, who believed he had more promise than any ballplayer he'd ever seen before.

Stengel constantly tried to motivate Mantle to reach his full potential. He seemed to regard him as a special project, a player whose talent was a work in progress. After Mantle's father's death, Stengel became Mickey's father figure—though baseball writer Robert Creamer described the pair as an angry father and his stubborn son. "He wanted me to be part of his legacy to the game," Mantle wrote of Stengel in *All My Octobers*, "to be the greatest player of all time, and he may have wanted that more than I wanted it for myself."

Mantle's own expectations of his abilities increased his anxiety. He wanted to win games with his bat and save games with his glove. When he failed, he blamed himself. As he often admitted, he was a poor loser.

Mantle found out about the birth of his first child over the Ebbets Field loudspeakers during an April 1953 exhibition game against the Dodgers. A month passed before he got home to meet his new son, Mickey Jr. Later that season, Merlyn and the baby moved to New Jersey, where the Mantle family could be together when the Yankees were home.

Mickey and Merlyn's children read a dispatch announcing Mantle's selection as the Most Valuable Player of 1962. From left to right are David, Merlyn, Dan, Mickey Jr., and Bill.

On April 17, against Washington, Mantle crushed a towering drive over the roof of Griffith Stadium. It landed 565 feet (172 meters) from home plate. In response to this, the term "tape measure home run" was coined to describe the longest drives. As usual, Mantle trotted around the bases with his head down so he wouldn't look like he was trying to embarrass the pitcher—and he almost ran right into Martin, who'd been on third base watching his friend's monumental hit.

Mantle made another lifelong friend that year, when a young pitcher named Whitey Ford rejoined the Yankees after completing his military service. Ford had been a rookie pitching sensation in 1950, going 9-1 in a half-season. He was a smart lefthander, born and raised in New York City. Mantle described him as funny, good-natured, and streetwise. Soon Ford, Mantle, and Martin became an inseparable trio.

However, after injuring both of his knees, Mantle missed a month of games. When he came back wearing a heavy knee brace, he convinced Stengel to let him play. His 21 home runs and 92 runs batted in helped the Yankees reach the World Series for a rematch with the Brooklyn Dodgers.

In Game 5, Mantle hit a grand slam home run, only the fourth player in series history to do so. Scrappy Martin batted .500 with 2 home runs and 8 runs batted in, and New York beat Brooklyn in 6 games to win their fifth straight championship—a record that may never be broken.

His Yankee teammates mob Mantle after he hit a grand slam in Game 5 of the 1953 World Series at Ebbets Field in Brooklyn, New York.

Mickey, Willie, and the Duke

The mid-1950s were exciting years for New York baseball fans. The Yankees, Giants, and Dodgers were all pennant contenders, and all three had future Baseball Hall of Famers playing center-field. The Dodgers' Duke Snider slugged at least 40 home runs for 5 straight seasons. The Giants' Willie Mays, with power and speed, was both graceful and electrifying. When it came to Mickey, Willie, and the Duke,

New York fans argued endlessly about who was the best ballplayer.

Despite another knee operation, Mantle's power increased over the next two seasons. In 1954, he hit 27 home runs. New York won 103 games but still finished second behind Cleveland. Even the Yankees couldn't win them all.

Still, the Yankees won the pennant again in 1955. Mantle hit a league-leading 37 home runs and became the first American Leaguer to hit home runs both left-handed and right-handed in one game. Unfortunately, he tore a thigh muscle in mid-September and missed the last two weeks of the season.

The Yanks again faced the Dodgers in the World Series. Brooklyn had played in six previous World Series without winning, including losses to the Yankees in 1941, 1947, 1949, 1952, and 1953. Mantle's injury limited his playing time, though he did hit his fifth series home run. With the series tied three-all, Johnny Podres pitched a brilliant shutout in Game 7, giving the Dodgers their first championship. This time, it was the Yankees who had to "Wait 'til next year."

A Year to Remember

It was worth the wait. Mantle began his explosive 1956 season with 2 long home runs on opening day—and 9 in his first 16 games. Stengel was certain that Mantle had more ability than any player he'd ever managed, and wondered if Mantle, now twenty-four years old, would finally realize his potential. The last five years of play had made Mantle a smarter ballplayer than ever before. He was also a proven hitter. As his phenomenal season continued, Stengel's curiosity vanished.

No one has ever hit a fair ball out of Yankee Stadium. On May 30, when Mantle clubbed a pitch from the Washington's Pedro Ramos high into the right-field sky, he came closer than anyone had before, or has since. It was a home run for sure—but how far would it go? Yankee Stadium is a huge ballpark, with three tall decks of stands. Before a 1974 renovation, the front of the upper deck had a metal-lattice façade hanging down from the roof. Mantle's towering drive hit that

Arrows show the path of Mantle's amazing 370-foot (113-meter) home run shot against the Senators on May 30, 1956. It struck the façade of the right field roof, 188 feet (57 meters) above the ground, and was just a few feet from leaving the ballpark.

façade—less than two feet (.610 meters) from the top.

Mantle seemed to have a chance at breaking Babe Ruth's 60 home-run record set in 1927. And he was quickly becoming one of America's best-known celebrities, thanks to television. The number of families with televisions had grown from a few thousand in 1946 to tens of millions by the mid-1950s. Starting in 1951, the World Series was broadcast live from coast to coast. With the Yankees reaching the series so often, millions of fans saw Mantle play. In cities everywhere, more fans watched local ballgames on television instead of listening to them on the radio.

Because of television, more people saw Mantle play in a single season than had watched Ruth in person during his entire career. Mantle's spectacular season propelled him into the spotlight like no athlete before him. He was a national media star, as well known as Elvis Presley. Pop singer Teresa Brewer recorded "I Love Mickey," a bouncy tune that literally sang the praises of Mantle's muscles and good looks.

Mantle just missed Ruth's record, but he became only the twelfth player to win the Triple Crown, leading the American League in batting average (.353), home runs (52), and runs batted in (130). In fact, he led both leagues—something only three other players have ever done.

With Yogi Berra's 30 home runs, Hank Bauer's 26, Moose Skowron's 23, and Whitey Ford's 19 wins, the Yankees won the pennant easily. The defending champion Dodgers paced

The Mick sings "I Love Mickey" with songwriter Teresa Brewer, who wrote the tune with Ruth Roberts and Bill Katz.

the National League again. Would the Yankees avenge their 1955 loss?

October Perfection

Playing like a team trying to prove their championship hadn't been a fluke, the Dodgers won the first two games at home. The Yanks roared back at Yankee Stadium, tying the series at two games apiece. Game 5 would be the last one in the Bronx. If the Yankees lost, they'd have to win two straight games in Brooklyn.

Why Do Today's Sluggers Hit More Homers?

Theories abound. Here are some key factors:

Lighter bats: Hitters gain bat speed and power.

Bigger players: Today's athletes are generally larger.

Smaller ballparks: Many big stadiums have been replaced by smaller traditional-style parks, where more fly balls reach the seats. Even Yankee Stadium shrank during its renovation in the mid-1970s.

Don Larsen pitched Game 5 for the Yankees, against intimidating Sal Maglie. Larsen, known more for partying than for his pitching, had been knocked out early during Game 2. The odds on October 8 favored the Dodgers.

For three innings, neither team managed a single base runner. In the bottom of the fourth inning, Mantle came to bat, hitting lefty. To keep him from pulling a home run down Yankee Stadium's short, 296-foot (90-meter) right field line, Maglie kept pitching to the outside corner. Mantle kept fouling them off. Then Maglie tried to fool him with an inside curveball. Mantle hit a line-drive homer just inside the right-field foul pole! The Yankees led 1–0.

In the fifth inning, Brooklyn first baseman Gil Hodges lined a drive into "Death Valley," the stadium's deep, left-center gap. Running at full speed, Mantle made a great backhanded catch to save the no-hitter, and maybe the game. The Yankees scored one more run. For the Dodgers, each inning was the same: no runs, hits, walks, or base runners.

Ninth inning. Two out. Dale Mitchell, a lifetime .314 hitter, came to bat for Brooklyn. With the count two balls, two strikes, Larsen threw a fastball across the outside corner. The umpire called strike three—and Yankee Stadium exploded with excitement. Larsen had pitched the one and only perfect game in World Series history. Then the Dodgers won Game 6 in Brooklyn, tying the series three-all. But the Yankees took Game 7 for their seventeenth world championship. With three more series home runs, Mantle now had eight.

Mantle seems to defy gravity as he leaps to catch the ball in a game against the White Sox on September 20, 1951.

After the season, Mantle received more honors—including the American League Most Valuable Player (MVP), *The Sporting News* player of the year award, and the Hickok Belt as Professional Athlete of the Year.

He was also flooded with business offers and invitations to make personal appearances, endorse products, and film television commercials. He became co-owner of the "Mickey Mantle" Holiday Inn in Oklahoma, and invested in a Dallas, Texas, bowling alley. To make traveling more convenient and to supervise the bowling alley, the Mantle family moved to Dallas, Texas.

In January, Mantle went to New York to discuss a new contract with team president George Weiss. The baseball business was very different back then. Teams owned their players and could trade or cut them at will. Unlike today, players weren't allowed to sell their talents to the highest bidder on the free-agent market. Multiyear contracts didn't exist; even superstars were signed one year at a time. And players didn't have professional agents to

Alvin Hickok *(right)* presents Mantle with the Rae Hickok jeweled belt for being named the professional athlete of the year on January 21, 1957.

negotiate their contracts for them. They had to make their own deals.

After his spectacular year, Mantle thought he deserved a superstar's salary. So he asked for $65,000, double his previous year's salary. Weiss rejected the amount, took a folder out of his desk, and showed it to Mantle. It contained reports from private detectives that the team had hired to document the late-night carousing of Mantle and his teammates. Years later,

Superstar Salary

Mantle's 1951 salary was $7,500—for the entire year. The Major League Baseball Players Association reports the minimum 2001 salary was $200,000 a year—twenty-six times what Mantle made!

The Yankees eventually paid Mantle $100,000 per year for his last six seasons. By comparison, current Yankee superstar Derek Jeter makes $18 million a year. That's more money per game— $111,111—than Mantle ever received for an entire season. The average ballplayer's salary in 2001 was about $2 million.

Mantle said that Weiss threatened to embarrass him by making the information public.

Mantle refused to surrender to blackmail and said he might just quit. Weiss threatened to trade him. Mantle needed the money to support his family, but the Yankees needed Mantle to keep winning. Though it appeared that the two were facing a stalemate, several days later, team co-owner Del Webb invited Mantle to spring training, where he signed for $65,000.

Wins and Losses

E arly in the 1957 season, with the team stumbling, Stengel benched Billy Martin in favor of rookie second baseman Bobby Richardson. Martin had always been one of Stengel's favorites, but Weiss didn't share that affection.

On May 15, Mantle, Ford, a few other teammates, and their wives were celebrating Martin's birthday at the famous Copacabana nightclub. As Mantle recalled, members of a bowling team at the next table heckled performer Sammy Davis Jr. onstage. After a heated verbal exchange between the bowlers and Martin, one heckler ended up on the floor near the club's cloakroom, knocked out cold.

Newspaper headlines the following day screamed about the brawl at the famous nightclub. The players involved all denied fighting, and Mantle thought a bouncer had

Mickey and pals pose for photos outside the New York City criminal courts building on June 24, 1957. A grand jury cleared his pal Hank Bauer in the Copacabana brawl. From left to right are Mantle, Billy Martin, Hank Bauer, and Mrs. Bauer.

thrown the only punch. The Yankees fined each of the players, and they were individually called to testify before a grand jury, but charges were dismissed. Weiss had long believed that Martin was a bad influence on Mantle, and this incident was the last straw. Within a month, Martin was traded to Kansas City.

In 1957, following his Triple Crown season, nervous pitchers walked Mantle 146 times. He still hit 34 home runs, batted a career-best .365, and won his second straight MVP award. The Yankees faced a different World Series opponent—the Milwaukee Braves, who beat the Yankees in seven games, led by their own star outfielder Hank Aaron and pitcher Lew Burdette. And Mantle suffered a new injury in Game 3, when Braves second baseman Red Schoendienst fell on him during an attempted pick-off. Despite off-season surgery, Mantle's shoulder was never the same. He never again hit with the same left-handed power as before.

Over the winter, New York's National League fans were shocked when both the Dodgers and Giants moved to California. It looked like there would never again be a New York Subway Series. (That changed when the New York Mets were born in 1962. But it would be another thirty-eight years until the 2000 Subway Series, when the Yanks beat the Mets four games to one.)

At contract-renewal time in early 1958, Mantle was astonished when Weiss tried to cut his salary by $5,000—because he'd failed to improve on his Triple Crown season. Eventually, Mantle got a $10,000 raise.

Mantle's sore shoulder, however, contributed to his slow start. Still, the Yankees raced through an early 25-6 streak and coasted to the pennant. Mantle led the league with 42 home runs and 129 walks. He even hit three inside-the-park homers within a month.

New York and Milwaukee played again in the 1958 World Series. Despite two more homers by Mantle, the Yankees fell behind three games to one. Afterward, they became the first team since the 1925 Pittsburgh Pirates to come back and win three straight games after trailing three to one.

A Year to Forget

Mantle's 1959 season began on a sour note. When Weiss again tried cutting his salary, Mantle refused to report to spring training. Eventually Weiss offered him a small raise, but the year was still a poor one in terms of baseball.

The Yankees stumbled early and never recovered. Mantle, accustomed to winning, took losing hard—and took his own failures even harder. For years, he'd prepared for every game by wrapping his sore knees in yards of bandage and tape. He was only twenty-eight, but the aches and pains of professional sports were taking a toll on his condition. In a game at Baltimore, Mantle hurried a throw and re-injured his shoulder. Soon after, a batting practice pitch hit his right hand and chipped a bone.

Mantle had his least productive season since 1951. Though he hit 31 home runs, his average skidded to .285, and he knocked in only 75 runs. He expected to hear booing from Yankee-haters on the road, but he didn't anticipate that New York fans would jeer him, too.

When sportswriters cornered him after a bad game, he'd turn sullen, then surly. His poor behavior and lack of diplomacy earned him a reputation as uncooperative. And when he fled mobs of fans demanding autographs, he was labeled as selfish.

But his teammates saw a different Mickey Mantle—a man who made an effort to be kind to rookies, who played without excuses when injured, and who hated to lose. They saw the guy that Stengel described to *Sports Illustrated*: "Here's what people don't realize . . . The knee bothers him and still he comes to me and says 'Let me play.' Sometimes I let him when I shouldn't . . . This boy loves to play baseball.'"

Loving the game wasn't easy for Mantle in 1959. The Yankees came in third, only the second time in his career when they hadn't finished first. Critics of sixty-nine-year-old Stengel complained he was too old, tired, and cranky to continue managing, even after nine pennants and seven championships in eleven years.

A Crushing Defeat

But Stengel was rejuvenated in 1960, along with his Yankees. Mantle also shined again—though not before another contract fight with Weiss. Mantle held out for ten days, then grudgingly settled for a $10,000 cut. But his bad mood persisted into the regular season, and he and the team suffered another slow start.

A player acquired in the off-season helped keep them afloat—twenty-five-year-old Roger Maris, a right fielder with a strong throwing arm. His left-handed swing and Yankee Stadium's short right-field fence were a great combination.

Mantle's poor play continued. After some embarrassing mistakes, Stengel benched his star in disgust. Jeers rolled down from the stands. And after Mantle caught the final out in one game, a rowdy fan ran onto the field and punched him in the jaw.

The Yankees ended the year with a fifteen-game winning streak and finished eight games ahead of Baltimore. Though Mantle's average slipped again, to .275, he led the league with 40 home runs. Maris hit 39 homers, knocked in a league-leading 112 runs, and won the American League's MVP award.

Their postseason opponents were the Pittsburgh Pirates, a team that hadn't played a World Series since 1927. Though the Bronx Bombers manhandled Pittsburgh by scores of 16–3, 10–0, and 12–0, the Pirates kept the series tied at three-all. In Game 7 at Pittsburgh, the Pirates jumped out to a 4–0 lead. By the eighth inning, the Yankees led 7–4. Then Pittsburgh got a break, when a sure double-play grounder skipped off a pebble and hit Yankee shortstop Tony Kubek in the throat. The Pirates scored five

Roger Maris *(left)* was voted MVP of the American League in 1961, and Mantle was the runner-up.

more runs, taking a 9–7 lead. The Yankees tied the game at 9–9, but Pirates second baseman Bill Mazeroski hit a game-winning home run.

Mantle had his best World Series, driving in 11 runs and batting .400. His 3 home runs gave him a lifetime series total of 14, one short of Ruth's record. But losing the series was a crushing disappointment, and Mantle cried on the flight back to New York. Stengel was fired. George Weiss retired a month later.

6 Chasing the Babe

B y 1961, Mantle was nearly thirty years old. Only a few teammates remained from his earliest seasons, including Ford and Berra. New Yankees manager Ralph Houk wanted Mantle to be a team leader, and sportswriters found him more relaxed and approachable.

The Yankees—and Maris—got off to a lackluster start. Mantle began the season with 4 homers in four early games. Maris didn't hit his first home run until the end of April, but then the ball started exploding off his bat. Over 38 games in May and June, he slugged 24 homers. Somehow, Mantle kept up. By July 19, Maris had 35 home runs, Mantle had 33, and both were ahead of Ruth's pace. Sportswriters called them the "M & M Boys," and the country had "Home Run Fever."

As Mantle and Maris continued to crush the ball, more reporters swarmed around them. Mantle had already challenged Ruth's record once, in 1956, and he was used to the pressure. But Maris had never weathered a press storm. He was only twenty-six, shy by nature, and more comfortable in his hometown of Fargo, North Dakota, than he'd ever be in New York.

By contrast, Mantle had come to enjoy city life. He still didn't care much for the news media, but he was accustomed to being a celebrity. Maris wasn't. The closer Maris came to Ruth's record, the more the press hounded him. Once surrounded, he'd give sullen responses to reporters' questions—if he answered them at all.

Some articles reported rumors of a feud between Mantle and Maris. In fact, Maris invited Mantle to move from his expensive Manhattan hotel to the Queens apartment Maris shared with reserve outfielder Bob Cerv. "He worried about how much it was costing me to live at the Hotel St. Moritz," Mantle wrote in *All My Octobers*. "He worried about the hours I kept and the night spots that were so convenient."

Soon Mantle and Maris were roommates as well as friends. Away from Manhattan's bright lights, the press left them alone. Off the field, Mantle helped Maris handle the pressure of the spotlight. On the field, Mantle thought their friendly rivalry helped them both play well.

Fan Favorite at Last

When it became clear that both Maris and Mantle had a shot at Ruth's record, a strange thing happened. Yankees fans began to root for Mantle more than ever before. Maris, unfortunately, was seen as an unsmiling outsider who didn't deserve to break one of the baseball's most hallowed records. If anyone was going to do it, they wanted that person to be Mantle. Fans finally realized "the Mick," as he was affectionately known, was someone special—the embodiment of Yankees tradition. Mantle got the cheers, and Maris got the jeers.

Though Maris was stressed, he kept hitting homers, as Mantle fell behind and then caught the flu. A New York doctor gave Mantle a botched injection in his right hip. The hip became badly

On and off the field, Mantle and Roger Maris were inseparable. Here they hold up a jersey with the number 44, honoring Mantle's forty-fourth home run that he hit against the Washington Senators in a game during the 1961 season.

infected, and doctors had to drain the abscess. Mantle spent the last week of the season in the hospital while Maris hit his sixty-first homer in the season's final game.

Maris also drove in a league-leading 142 runs and won his second straight MVP Award. Mantle had the second-best year of his career, with 54 home runs, a .317 average, and 128 runs batted in.

During the World Series against Cincinnati, Mantle's hip infection kept him on the bench until Game 3. With his open wound carefully bandaged, Mantle went 0 for 4. In Game 4, he lined a shot off the left-center-field wall. It should have been an easy double, but the pain forced him to stop at first with blood running down his leg, staining his uniform. Mantle sat out the rest of the series, but the Yankees beat the Reds easily for their nineteenth world championship.

Mantle thought the 1961 Yankees were the best team with whom he'd ever played, and Maris breaking Ruth's record the greatest thing he'd ever witnessed. Unfortunately for Maris, many fans didn't share Mantle's opinion.

"In a curious way, Maris made me more popular in New York than I had ever been [before]," Mantle wrote in *All My Octobers*. "They wouldn't forgive Roger for not being Babe Ruth. They finally forgave me for not being Joe DiMaggio. For the first time, they saw me as an underdog . . . playing hurt. In a way I had not heard before, they cheered me for what I did and what I might have done."

From then on, Mantle could do no wrong. And Maris could do nothing right. Throughout 1962, fans sneered at Maris in every ballpark, so much so that he sometimes wished he'd never broken Ruth's record at all.

Heart of the Yankees

During an unimportant ballgame in May, Mantle managed to injure both legs on one play while trying to beat out an infield hit. He missed the next month, though he tried to handle his situation with humor. Walter Bingham wrote in *Sports Illustrated*, "At least 50 times a day, Mantle was asked about the condition of his legs. Finally he got a piece of paper on which he printed: 'Slight improvement. Be back in two weeks. So don't ask.' He taped the paper to his chest."

The Yankees won the pennant again, and beat the San Francisco Giants in a seven-game World Series for their twentieth championship. Though he missed a quarter of the season, Mantle still batted .321 with 30 homers and won his third MVP award—an award that proved he was the heart of the Yankees in a way that transcended statistics.

In 1963, Mantle's salary was $100,000. He showed why he was worth it on the night of May 22, against Kansas City at Yankee Stadium. Batting lefty, he crushed what he said was the hardest ball he ever hit. It zoomed toward the glare of the lights above the roof, still rising when it slammed into the same façade as his 1956 moon-shot had. Once again, he just missed hitting a ball out of cavernous Yankee Stadium.

Just two weeks later, on a damp Baltimore night, Orioles third baseman Brooks Robinson hit a long drive to center. Unlike most ballparks, Memorial Stadium didn't have a "warning track" to alert fielders nearing the outfield wall. As Mantle reached for the ball, he ran out of space. His spikes caught in the chain-link fence and he fell, breaking his left foot and injuring his knee. He was carried off the field and wondered if his career was over.

After missing 61 games, Mantle returned. New York had already lost the first game of a Yankee Stadium doubleheader against Baltimore and trailed 10-9 in the bottom of the seventh. As Mantle appeared from the dugout to pinch-hit, he got the loudest cheers of his life. On the second pitch, he hit a homer. The crowd went wild. The Yankees won that game and easily won the pennant, despite injuries that sidelined both Mantle and Maris.

New York played the Dodgers in the World Series, their first rematch since Brooklyn had moved west. Behind dominating pitching, Los Angeles won the first three games. New York faced elimination. Game 4 at Dodger Stadium was a battle of pitching aces—Whitey Ford against Sandy Koufax. Ford gave up the first run in the fifth. In the seventh, Mantle tied the game—and Ruth's record—with his fifteenth series home

Mantle misses a pitch from Dodger pitcher Sandy Koufax by a long shot during Game 1 of the 1963 World Series. The Yankees were swept in four games, and Koufax allowed only four runs in that season's games against the Bronx Bombers.

run. The Dodgers scored an unearned run in the bottom of the seventh, Koufax held on, and the Dodgers swept the series, allowing just four Yankee runs in four games.

A week later, Houk was promoted to team vice president, and Yogi Berra replaced him as manager. The sun was already setting on the Yankees' four-decade dynasty.

A Last Hurrah

Although he was well liked, Berra had a hard time commanding respect as a leader. As Mantle observed, Berra had rules, but he didn't enforce them. The Yankees languished in third place, and Berra's job was in jeopardy—until they went 22-6 in September, clinching the pennant by a small margin. Mantle missed nineteen games but still led the team with 35 homers and 111 runs.

The Yankees played the St. Louis Cardinals in the World Series. Mantle rose to the occasion, almost as if he knew this would be his final championship. With the series even at one game apiece, Game 3 was tied 1–1 going into the bottom of the ninth, with Mantle due to lead off.

On his way to the plate, he told Elston Howard he planned to end the game with one swing—and he did, slugging the first pitch into the upper deck. His sixteenth series home run broke Ruth's lifetime record!

The series came down to Game 7 in St. Louis. Mantle hit a three-run homer, but the Cardinals won the game and the championship. Mantle's final Series was one of his best. He hit .333 with 3 home runs and 8 runs batted in.

In mid-season, the CBS television network had purchased the Yankees. Although it came as no surprise when the new corporate owners fired Berra, the hiring of Cardinals manager Johnny Keane as his replacement was a shock.

The Dynasty Crumbles

By 1965, Mantle's legs were in such poor shape that he could barely run, but his troubled teammates needed him. The Yankees' farm system—once superior but now neglected—had no future superstars to offer.

Keane had been hired specifically to impose the sort of discipline that Berra couldn't,

Yankee manager Yogi Berra presents Mantle with an honorary bat in September 1954 to celebrate his passing 2,000 hits in his career, the fifth Yankee to do so.

including a ban on late-night partying. When Mantle defied him, Keane attempted to make an example of his behavior by running him ragged. The sight of their fading star chasing one fly ball after another did not endear Keane to Mantle's teammates.

Ultimately, the season was a disaster. For the first time in forty years, the Yankees finished under .500, buried in sixth place. Mantle's sore shoulder and legs forced him to move to left field, where he'd have less ground to cover and shorter throws. He hit only 19 homers and batted .255.

Following the season, Mantle hurt his shoulder during a family game of touch football. After surgery, he reported to spring training. The Yankees were going nowhere, but he needed the salary, still enjoyed the cheering, and couldn't imagine not being part of a team. Mantle wasn't ready to retire. *Sports Illustrated* writer Jack Mann described Mantle as "the one-man orthopedic ward." Teammates and opponents wondered how long he could continue playing.

Keane was fired three weeks into the season. Houk took over again, but the magic was gone. The Yankees finished last for the first time since 1912. Playing just 108 games, Mantle still hit 23 home runs, with a .288 average.

Twilight of a Superstar

By the 1967 and '68 seasons, Mantle could no longer play the outfield. To save wear on his battered legs and shoulder, Houk moved him to first base. Ford had retired. Maris, always miserable in New York, had been traded. Virtually all Mantle's other teammates from the glory days were gone, too. The ballpark just wasn't the same anymore.

With no pennant at stake, Mantle was playing for his place in history and reaching important milestones, including his 500th home run in May. He was a legend at the end of the line, universally cheered at every ballpark in the league. Even opposing players treated him with astonishing respect. Veterans told rookies not to take advantage of his lack of mobility by bunting down the first-base line.

He climbed higher on the all-time home run list, passing Ted Williams at 521, then tying Jimmy Foxx at 534. Mantle's next homer came in Detroit—with a little help from Tigers pitcher Denny McLain.

The Tigers had already clinched the 1968 pennant, and McLain was about to win 31 games. When Mantle limped up to bat late in the game, McLain told his catcher he was going to let Mantle hit one. Not quite believing what he'd heard, Mantle took a fat fastball for a strike. Next pitch, another meaty fastball, and Mantle fouled it off. The third pitch was a fastball down the middle, and this time

Mantle watches the ball he just hit fly into the stands, marking his 500th home run during a game in May 1967. The Mick would make it to 536 before retiring.

Mantle got it—home run 535 into the upper deck. When he hit number 536 on September 20 at Yankee Stadium, it would be his last.

After winter, Mantle went to Florida and tried to work out. But his aching legs confirmed what he already knew. At thirty-eight years old, Mantle announced he was retiring. He could no longer perform the way he once could. Mantle's biggest regret was that his final-season batting average of .237 had dragged his lifetime average just below .300.

Mantle holds up a jersey with his number 7. In his honor, the number was retired when he left baseball in 1969, meaning that no other Yankee would ever sport that number.

Redemption

On June 8, 1969, the Yankees honored Mantle at "Mickey Mantle Day" and retired his famous number 7. Mantle told the crowd that playing his entire career in Yankee Stadium was the best thing that could happen to a ballplayer. And he finally understood how the dying Lou Gehrig could have said on the same field thirty years before that he was the luckiest man on the face of the earth.

But Mantle had a difficult time finding a new direction for his life. He'd said he wanted to spend more time with his sons, but for their entire lives, he'd been home only four or five months out of each year. Now, back in Dallas, with the chance to be a full-time father to four young boys, he wasn't sure how to do it well.

He had to support his family without his Yankee salary. Business investments, including the Dallas bowling alley and a Mickey Mantle Country Cookin' restaurant chain, hadn't been successful. He also worked as a Yankee coach, as a sports commentator, and in public relations.

But Mantle missed playing ball so much that he'd have a recurring nightmare in which he arrived outside Yankee Stadium, wearing his uniform, hearing his name over the loudspeakers, then getting stuck trying to squeeze through a hole in the fence while his teammates waited for him. Afterward, he'd wake up in a cold sweat.

Fame and Misfortune

In 1974, Mantle was elected to the Baseball Hall of Fame in Cooperstown, New York, chosen in his first year of eligibility. Whitey Ford, who had just missed selection the year before, was also elected. The two old friends were inducted together, with Casey Stengel there to congratulate two of his favorite players.

Meanwhile, Mantle's sons had become troubled teenagers. They had problems in school, and used alcohol and drugs. In 1977, nineteen-year-old Billy was diagnosed with Hodgkin's disease. Mantle, who had lived to be older than his father and uncles had, wondered why the cancer that cursed his family had skipped him only to strike his son. After a long, painful battle, however, Billy's disease went into remission.

During the 1980s, the baby boom generation of children who'd grown up during the 1950s became nostalgic for symbols of their childhood. Things that might once have been thrown away—including old baseball cards, yearbooks, and pennants—had suddenly become valuable collectibles. At baseball memorabilia shows all over the country, vendors sold souvenirs old and new, and retired ballplayers were paid to sign autographs.

Thanks to this nostalgia boom, Mantle was in great demand. He was paid thousands of dollars to sign autographs at card shows. Memorabilia companies paid him thousands more to pre-sign balls, bats, uniform shirts, and photos. Mantle made more in a weekend than he had made for an entire season playing ball! Though still uncomfortable with public speaking, he'd become a charming storyteller. And there were plenty of

While in retirement, Mantle found that classic memorabilia bearing his name, such as the objects in this display case, could fetch thousands of dollars.

audiences who wanted to hear about his glory days. With a growing sense of humor, he often poked fun at himself in the process.

Just as he'd finally achieved financial security for his family, that family was falling apart. His grown sons all had alcohol and drug problems. Unable to connect with them when they were young, Mantle and his adult sons found something in common: They became drinking buddies. Even Merlyn had become a heavy drinker during her marriage to Mickey.

(Mantle and his wife separated in the late 1980s, though they never divorced.)

"Baseball didn't turn me into a drunk," Mantle wrote in *A Hero All His Life*, "although I believe now that leaving it speeded up the process . . . My drinking problems grew gradually . . . each year . . . When I retired . . . my drinking became more frequent, and by the 1980s, I was a drunk."

Tarnished Hero

Mantle knew his life had been filled with great experiences, but he thought he'd wasted much of his natural talent. After baseball, nothing felt natural. When writers described him as a folk hero, Mantle didn't feel like a hero of any kind.

When he drank to overcome his shyness, he believed he was "the life of the party," Mantle told *Sports Illustrated* in 1994. "But as it turned out, nobody could stand to be around me."

"I am embarrassed by what I did when I drank," he wrote in *A Hero All His Life*, "the foul language, the rudeness, having to face people the next day whom I didn't remember insulting the night before."

The more he traveled, the more lonely nights he spent in hotels—and the more he drank. Inevitably, drinking affected his health. He developed an ulcer, had memory blackouts and panic attacks, and hated to be home alone.

He was an alcoholic, but he couldn't admit it. Friends begged him to stop drinking, but he couldn't do it on his own and wasn't yet ready to get help. Merlyn was the first person in the Mantle family to try to stop drinking. Then, in 1993, Mantle's son Danny entered a California drug and alcohol treatment center founded by former first lady Betty Ford. Mrs. Ford had overcome her own alcohol and prescription-drug abuse problems and wanted to help others.

In December 1993, Mantle's doctor told him that years of alcohol abuse had damaged his liver so badly that his next drink might be his last. Mantle was afraid fans would remember him as a drunk, instead of as a great ballplayer. He realized he was killing himself. He knew he needed help to win what he called the greatest game of his life.

At a 1994 news conference held at the restaurant he owned, Mantle told reporters that he was looking forward to going to fantasy baseball camp that fall, this time clean and sober for the first time in years.

Getting Sober

Mantle received that help during a monthlong stay at the Betty Ford Center, where group therapy sessions helped him understand his unexpressed love for his father. For the first time, he was able to admit how his drinking had hurt his family. He confronted how badly he felt about himself and his past mistakes.

Many medical experts believe alcoholism is a disease of addiction, and that some people have a genetic tendency to develop or exhibit addictive personalities. Because alcoholics' bodies crave alcohol, it's hard for them to control their intake of alcohol. Alcoholics cannot quit after just one drink. But drinking is still a choice, even for an alcoholic. For those who choose to stop, treatment centers and support groups can help.

When Mantle came out of rehab, sober for the first time in forty years, he faced the scary prospect of a changed way of life. He swore that he would never drink alcohol again. That determination was soon tested by grief. His son Billy had been in and out of drug treatment programs and had undergone heart surgery in 1993. Just a few weeks after Mantle's stay at Betty Ford, Billy died of a heart attack. He was only thirty-six years old. Overwhelmed with guilt, Mantle wondered how his son's life would have been different if he'd been a better father.

Still, Mantle kept his pledge of sobriety, and looked ahead. For years, he told *Sports Illustrated,* "I lived the life of somebody I didn't know; a cartoon character. From now on, Mickey Mantle is going to be a real person. I still can't remember much of the last ten years, but from what I've been told, I really don't want those memories. I'm looking forward to the memories I'll have in the next ten years."

He planned to cut back on travel and to spend more time with his family. Mantle also wanted to help other aging ballplayers who were going through tough times. He wanted to speak with teenagers about the dangers of drugs and alcohol. Sadly, he'd only have another eighteen months to be the Mickey Mantle he wanted to be.

In May 1995, Mantle checked into Baylor University Medical Center in Dallas with severe stomach pains. Years of drinking had destroyed his liver, and he had developed liver cancer. He needed a liver transplant. It might have been weeks or months before he got an organ, but his condition worsened quickly. With only days to live, he received the first available liver on June 8.

Mick's Last Inning

During the operation, surgeons found that Mantle's cancer had spread. He was given medication to keep his body from rejecting the new liver and chemotherapy to fight the cancer.

Three weeks after his transplant, Mantle went home. Weak after losing 30 pounds (13.3 kg), he appeared at a July 11 press conference with his doctors. He pointed to himself and asked kids to use him as a kind of reverse role model. "Don't be like me," he said to the news media.

Everyone knew he was referring to the ravaging affects of alcohol, which had abused his body and mind. But on that day in Baylor's pressroom, Mantle became the right kind of role model—bravely facing his flaws with honesty instead of shame, worthy of admiration.

Mantle learned firsthand that there aren't enough organs for all the sick people who need transplants. He wanted to use his fame to promote awareness of organ-donor programs and even came up with a campaign slogan: "Be a hero, be a donor."

But Mantle's cancer proved unstoppable. He went back into the hospital on July 28. Too sick to appear on live television, he videotaped a short message asking people to become donors. His

Dr. Robert Goldstein, a transplant surgeon, watches Mantle on videotape during a news conference in which the Yankee legend announced that his cancer had spread to his right lung.

doctors said that he promoted organ donation and transplants more than anyone ever had before.

A week later, the doctors told him they couldn't save him. Mantle's family alerted his former teammates. On short notice, Whitey Ford, Bobby Richardson, Hank Bauer, and others from those famous Yankee championship seasons came to visit, and to say good-bye.

Mantle faced his last days with peaceful dignity. "His disposition was remarkable," Dr. Daniel DeMarco told the *New York Times*.

"Somebody is lying on their deathbed, and you disturb them, and the first thing they do is smile at you. I've never really seen anyone do that. And then he would . . . shake your hand. It's something I'll never forget."

Whitey Ford had brought a gift—a baseball signed by that season's Yankees, inscribed with get-well wishes. The ball was next to Mantle when he died early Sunday morning, August 13, 1995. He was sixty-three years old.

A Hero Again

There was a game at Yankee Stadium that sunny afternoon. The Yankees wore black armbands on their uniforms. Almost 46,000 fans and players stood for a moment of silence. The crowd gave him one more standing ovation.

Fifteen hundred mourners packed the church for Mantle's funeral in Dallas, Texas, broadcast live on ESPN television. In his eulogy, NBC sportscaster Bob Costas called Mantle "a fragile hero . . . too honest to regard himself as some kind of deity."

"There was greatness in him, but vulnerability, too," Costas said. "In the last year, Mickey Mantle, always so hard on himself, finally came to accept and appreciate the distinction between a role model and a hero. The first he often was not, the second he always will be." He talked about Mantle's final months of courage, and "the sheer grace of that ninth inning, the humility . . . the total absence of self-pity, the simple eloquence and honesty of his pleas to others to take heed of his mistakes . . . Our last memories of Mickey Mantle are as heroic as the first. None of us, Mickey included, would want to be held to account for every moment of our lives. But how many of us could say that our best moments were as magnificent as his?"

Costas also remembered a funny story Mantle often told about a dream in which he dies and shows up at the Pearly Gates. Saint Peter tells him they can't let him into Heaven because he hadn't always been good. "But before you go," Saint Peter says, "God wants to know if you'd sign these six dozen balls."

The plaque that commemorates Mickey Mantle at the Baseball Hall of Fame

Comparing Sluggers

Even for people who dislike math, comparing statistics is part of the fun of being a fan. Great sluggers not only hit a lot of home runs, they hit them more often than other players do. Here's a chart comparing Mickey Mantle to other sluggers past and present:

Player	Career HR total	At-bats per HR
Hank Aaron	755	16.37
Babe Ruth	714	11.76
Willie Mays	660	16.48
Frank Robinson	586	17.07
Mark McGwire	583	10.61
Harmon Killebrew	573	14.22
Barry Bonds*	567	13.98
Reggie Jackson	563	17.42
Mike Schmidt	548	15.24
Mickey Mantle	536	15.11
Ken Griffey Jr.*	460	14.6
Sammy Sosa*	450	14.37

(* indicates active players after 2001 season)

In Ruth's 60-home-run season, he averaged 1 homer per 9 at-bats. Maris hit 61 at a rate of 1 per 9.67 at-bats. When Mantle hit 54 homers, he averaged 1 every 9.51 at-bats. When Mark McGwire broke Maris's record with 70 in 1998, he averaged 1 homer per 7.27 at-bats. And when Barry Bonds hit 73 to set a new record in 2001, he hit homers at the amazing rate of 1 per 6.52 at-bats.

Epitaph: Mantle's Place in Baseball History

By statistics alone, Mickey Mantle wasn't the greatest ballplayer of all time, or even the best ballplayer of his era. Willie Mays and Hank Aaron both played longer, with more home runs and higher batting averages. But Mantle's greatness goes beyond statistics. He retired third on the list of all-time home run hitters. His 2,401 games are more than any player currently in a Yankees uniform has. Some of Mantle's World Series records may stand forever, because few players will ever appear in as many World Series games as Mantle did. If you ever go to Yankee Stadium, be sure to visit Monument Park. Mantle's bronze memorial plaque, dedicated soon after his death, calls him "A great teammate . . . a magnificent Yankee who left a legacy of unequaled courage." Mantle deserves to be remembered for his accomplishments as a player, and for his courage as a person.

Mickey Mantle's Career Statistics

Regular Season:

Year	Team	G	AB	R	H	2B	3B	HR	RBI	Avg
1951	NY (A)	96	341	61	91	11	5	13	65	.267
1952	NY (A)	142	549	94	171	37	7	23	87	.311
1953	NY (A)	127	461	105	136	24	3	21	92	.295
1954	NY (A)	146	543	129	163	17	12	27	102	.300

Year	Team	G	AB	R	H	2B	3B	HR	RBI	Avg
1955	NY (A)	147	517	121	158	25	11	37	99	.306
1956	NY (A)	150	533	132	188	22	5	52	130	.353
1957	NY (A)	144	474	121	173	28	6	34	94	.365
1958	NY (A)	150	519	127	158	21	1	42	97	.304
1959	NY (A)	144	541	104	154	23	4	31	75	.285
1960	NY (A)	153	527	119	145	17	6	40	94	.275
1961	NY (A)	153	514	132	163	16	6	54	128	.317
1962	NY (A)	123	377	96	121	15	1	30	89	.321
1963	NY (A)	65	172	40	54	8	0	15	35	.314
1964	NY (A)	143	465	92	141	25	2	35	111	.303
1965	NY (A)	122	361	44	92	12	1	19	46	.255
1966	NY (A)	108	333	40	96	12	1	23	56	.288
1967	NY (A)	144	440	63	108	17	0	22	55	.245
1968	NY (A)	144	435	57	103	14	1	18	54	.237
Totals		2,401	8,102	1,677	2,415	344	72	536	1,509	.298

World Series:

Year	Opp	G	AB	R	H	2B	3B	HR	RBI	Avg
1951	NY (N)	2	5	1	1	0	0	0	0	.200
1952	Bkn	7	29	5	10	1	1	2	3	.345
1953	Bkn	6	24	3	5	0	0	2	7	.208
1955	Bkn	3	10	1	2	0	0	1	1	.200
1956	Bkn	7	24	6	6	1	0	3	4	.250
1957	Mil	6	19	3	5	0	0	1	2	.263
1958	Mil	7	24	4	6	0	1	2	3	.250
1960	Pit	7	25	8	10	1	0	3	11	.400
1961	Cin	2	6	0	1	0	0	0	0	.167
1962	SF	7	25	2	3	1	0	0	0	.120
1963	LA	4	15	1	2	0	0	1	1	.133
1964	StL	7	24	8	8	2	0	3	8	.333
Totals		65	230	42	59	6	2	18	40	.257

Lifetime World Series Records:

Most home runs:	18
Most runs batted in:	40
Most runs scored:	42
Most walks:	43
Most strikeouts:	54

MICKEY MANTLE *TIMELINE*

1931	Mickey Mantle is born during the Great Depression.
1947	Sixteen-year-old Mantle plays shortstop for the Whiz Kids, a Ban Johnson league, drawing local attention.
1949	Mantle signs a contract with the New York Yankees for $1,500.
1951	Mantle says good-bye to his parents as he heads to New York to play professional ball. He slumps during his rookie season. Mantle and Merlyn Johnson are married.
1952	Mantle's father dies on May 6 and Mickey plays in a Yankees game that day in his honor.
1953	Mickey and Merlyn Mantle have their first child, a son, Mickey Jr. Mantle hits a grand slam home run in Game 5 of the 1953 World Series.
1956	Mantle scores big as the Yankees win the World Series and is offered endorsement contracts. The Mantle family moves to Dallas, Texas.

⚾	**1957**	Mantle is involved in an infamous brawl at the Copacabana nightclub in New York.
⚾	**1959**	The Yankees face a slump and Mantle has his worst season since 1951, though his Series play is phenomenal: He bats .400.
⚾	**1961**	Fans applaud the Mick like never before as he competes to beat Babe Ruth's home-run record. Mantle is forced out due to injury.
⚾	**1963**	Mantle beats Babe Ruth's lifetime record with a sixteenth Series home run. It is his final World Series.
⚾	**1969**	The Yankees honor a retired Mantle at "Mickey Mantle Day" and retire his famous number 7.
⚾	**1974**	Mantle is admitted to the Baseball Hall of Fame.
⚾	**1995**	Mantles dies of cancer on August 12, surrounded by family.

Glossary

draft   A government system for selecting people for military service.

eulogy   A speech of praise given at someone's funeral.

exhibition game   A game that doesn't count in regular-season standings or records; usually played during spring training.

farm team   A minor league team where future major league players are developed.

grand slam   A home run hit with the bases loaded.

Great Depression   The period of economic hardship and widespread unemployment during the 1930s.

heckle   To harass or annoy someone with unwanted comments.

memorabilia   Objects that remind us of someone or something enjoyable.

MVP   Most valuable player.

nostalgia   A longing for experiences and events from the past.

perfect game   A complete game in which a pitcher allows no opponents at all to reach base on hits, errors, or walks.

pick-off   When the team in the field tries to catch a runner taking a big lead off any base.

rookie   A first-year player.

sandlot team   An informally organized non-professional team that usually plays together, but not in an official league; so named because many of these teams used to play in vacant lots rather than on actual baseball fields at parks or schools.

scout   A person who seeks out talented young players to be signed by major league teams.

Subway Series   The name given to a World Series played between two New York City teams because the city subway system links New York's five boroughs (or counties).

switch-hitter   A batter who can hit either right-handed or left-handed.

For More Information

National Baseball Hall of Fame and Museum
  25 Main Street
   P.O. Box 590
    Cooperstown, NY 13326
    (888) Hall-of-Fame (425-5633)
    Web site:
    http://www.baseballhalloffame.org

  New York Yankees
  Yankee Stadium
  161st Street and River Avenue
 Bronx, NY 10452
Web site: http://www.yankees.com

For Further Reading

Mantle, Merlyn, and Mickey Herskowitz.
A Hero All His Life. New York:
HarperCollins Publishers, 1996.

Mantle, Mickey, and Mickey Herskowitz.
All My Octobers. New York:
HarperCollins Publishers, 1994.

Mantle, Mickey, and Robert W. Creamer.
The Quality of Courage. Nebraska, WI:
University of Nebraska Press, 1999.

Robinson, Ray, and Christopher Jennison.
*Pennants and Pinstripes: The New York
Yankees 1903–2002*. New York: Viking
Press, 2002.

Sweet, Ozzie, and Larry Canale. *Mickey
Mantle: The Yankee Years: The Classic
Photography of Ozzie Sweet*. New York:
Antique Trader, 1998.

Bibliography

Creamer, Robert. *Sports Illustrated Presents Mantle Remembered*. New York: Warner Books, 1995.

Faulkner, David. *The Last Hero: The Life of Mickey Mantle*. New York: Simon & Schuster, 1995.

Mantle, Merlyn, and Mickey Herskowitz. *A Hero All His Life*. New York: HarperCollins Publishers, 1996.

Mantle, Mickey, and Herb Gluck. *The Mick: An American Hero: The Legend and the Glory*. New York: Jove/Berkley Publishing Group, 1986.

Mantle, Mickey, and Mickey Herskowitz. *All My Octobers*. New York: HarperCollins Publishers, 1994.

Myerson, Allen R. "Teammates Lifted Spirits in Final Days." *The New York Times*, August 14, 1995, pp. C-1, C-5.

Index

About the Author

Born in New York, Howard Weinstein became a Yankee fan at age seven in 1961, the memorable season when Mickey Mantle and Roger Maris chased the ghost of Babe Ruth. During his childhood, he was lucky enough to see the Mick play at Yankee Stadium. Mantle inspired him to make an unsuccessful attempt to become a switch-hitter. Weinstein has written thirteen books, including six *Star Trek* novels. Still a Yankee fan, he now lives in Maryland with wife Susan and their two dogs, Callie and Mickey, named in honor of Mantle.

Photo Credits

Cover © Bettmann/Corbis; pp. 4, 8, 29, 58, 61, 83, 84, 88, 91, 95 © AP/Wide World Photos; p. 6 © Topps Company; pp. 11, 12, 21, 26, 32, 37, 40, 43, 46, 48, 51, 53, 56, 71, 76–77, 80 © Bettmann/Corbis; p. 16 © Timepix; pp. 25, 67 © Hulton-Archive/Getty Images; p. 98 © Allsport/Getty Images.

Editor

Joann Jovinelly

Series Design and Layout

Geri Giordano